Forgiving & Being Forgiven

R. Jay Waggoner

EMMAUS
WORLDWIDE

Developed as a study course by Emmaus Correspondence School, founded in 1942.

Mission
Glorify God by providing biblically sound resources and structured
study materials that teach people from every nation to accept Christ as
their Savior and Lord, grow in Christ and share their faith with others.

Forgiving & Being Forgiven
R. Jay Waggoner

Published by:
Emmaus Worldwide
PO Box 1028
Dubuque, IA 52004-1028
phone: (563) 585-2070
email: info@emmausworldwide.org
website: www.EmmausWorldwide.org

First Edition 2014 (AK '14), 1 Unit
Reprinted 2015 (AK '14), 1 Unit
Reprinted 2019 (AK '14), 1 Unit
Revised 2020 (AK '20), 1 Unit
Revised 2023 (AK '23), 1 Unit

ISBN 978-1-59387-200-7

Code: FBF

Printed in the United States of America

Course Description

Forgiving & Being Forgiven concisely presents what the Bible teaches about a crucial matter in every relationship—the need to forgive one another. The author sets this study in the context of some real-life experiences and the research of respected Christian experts in the field. He draws principles from the teachings of Christ Himself and other related Bible texts to make pertinent and practical applications to this challenging aspect of our lives.

Whether you need to forgive someone who has offended you or you need to be forgiven, this short course is your guide to repairing the damage.

Lessons You Will Study

Student Instructions

This Emmaus course is designed to help you know God through a better understanding of the Bible and know it applies to your life. However, this course can never take the place of the Bible itself. The Bible is inexhaustible, and no course can give the full meaning of its truth. If simply studying this course is the end goal, it will become an obstacle to your growth; if it is used to inspire and equip you for your own personal study of the Bible, then it will achieve its goal. As you study the Bible using this course, prayerfully ask God to reveal His truth to you in a powerful way.

Course Sections

This course has three parts: the *lessons*, the *exams* and the *answer sheet*.

The Lessons

Each lesson is written to help explain truths from the Bible. Read each lesson through at least twice—once to get a general idea of its content, then again, slowly, looking up any Bible references given. You should always have your Bible opened to the verses or passage being studied. It is important that you read the Bible passages referenced, as some questions in the exams may be based on the Bible text.

To look up a Bible verse, keep in mind that passages in the Bible are listed by book, chapter, and verse. For instance, 2 Peter 1:21 refers to the second book of Peter, chapter 1, and verse 21. At the beginning of every Bible, there is a table of contents which lists the names of the books of the Bible and tells the page number on which each book begins. For practice, look up 2 Peter in the table of contents, turn to the page number listed, then find the chapter and verse.

The Exams

At the end of each lesson, there is an exam to assess your knowledge of the course material and the Bible passages. The exams contain multiple choice and/or True/False (T/F) questions. After you have studied a lesson, complete the exam for that lesson by recording your answers on the exam sheet that has been provided. If you have difficulty answering the questions, re-read the lesson or use the Bible as a reference.

Please note, it is best not to answer the questions based on what you *think* or have *always believed*. The questions are designed to find out if you understand the material in the course and the Bible.

What Do You Say?

In addition to the multiple choice section, each exam also contains a *What Do You Say?* question. These questions are designed for your personal reflection and to help you express your ideas and feelings as you process the lesson's content.

The Answer Sheet

Use the answer sheet provided by your group leader or instructor. When you have determined the right answer to a question on an exam, fill in the corresponding letter on the answer sheet. If you do not have someone who could provide an answer sheet, you can download one at www.emmausworldwide.org/answersheets

If you are an Emmaus Homeschool student, please disregard any further instructions.

Submitting the Answer Sheet

When you have answered all the exam questions on the answer sheet, check them carefully. Fill in your contact information and submit your completed answer sheet to your group leader or instructor or the organization from which you received it.

OPTION 1: Send to your group leader or instructor

If you know your group leader or instructor, give them your completed answer sheet or mail it to the address listed here (if blank, go to option 2).

OPTION 2: Send to Emmaus Worldwide's head office

If no address is listed above, or if you do not know if you have a group leader or instructor and are unsure of where to send your answer sheet, choose one of the following:

MAIL the exam sheet to

Please return to
Emmaus Bible School UK
28—30 Larkhill Lane
Liverpool
Merseyside. L13 9BR
Tel: 0151 352 9269
www.emmausuk.com

EMAIL the exam sheet to

Exams@EmmausWorldwide.org

Receiving Your Results

You will receive back your graded exam sheet (through the same method it was submitted, either mail or email), including your final grade and a personal response from your group leader or instructor or a representative of Emmaus Worldwide.

LESSON 1

When We Are At Fault

Our relationships are vital. Relationships with other human beings are the foundation stones of our society. Relationships are crucial to the success and wellbeing of families, businesses, churches, and communities. They are also vital to the wellbeing of every individual. God created within us the need to interact with other human beings. Dr. Paul Faulkner, in his book *Making Things Right When Things Go Wrong*, cites an amazing study that connects health and wellbeing with social interaction:

> Lisa Berkman and her colleagues at the University of California in Berkeley made an intensive study of 7,000 adults over a period of nine years. They found that people with weak social ties to others had a two-to-five times higher death rate than folks with strong social ties. That's a startling statistic! They're saying that a person with few or no friends is far more likely to die prematurely than a person with a lot of friends. This finding held true, regardless of whether the person smoked, drank, exercised, jogged, or was overweight.[1]

Relationships are certainly crucial to the individual. Furthermore, one can only wonder what the effect of broken relationships may be on a whole generation of young people. According to an article in *USA Today* in 1999, 23 percent of U.S. children were living in single-parent households in 1960, and by 1990 that figure had increased to 42 percent.[2]

In spite of their connection to our health and wellbeing, and in spite of their importance to society in general, relationships often fail. John C. Maxwell, in his book *Be a People Person* (pp. 118-119), identifies a common process that relationships go through before ending in separation. He says that relationships begin with a **honeymoon stage,** in which the parties are temporarily blinded to the negative traits of the other person in the excitement of finding someone who meets a need in their lives. The honeymoon stage is followed by the **specific irritation stage,** in which reality sets in and negative irritating traits are noticed. The third stage is the **general discomfort stage,** in which specific irritations pile up and the parties begin to express their discomfort.

The **try harder stage** follows, in which the parties increase efforts to solve their problems. Unfortunately, by this point it is often hard for them to separate the problem from the person. The **exhaustion stage** follows, when the parties tend to throw up their hands and quit on the relationship. **Separation** is the final stage.[3] Simply put, every unresolved irritation brings about a degree of emotional distance between two people. With each irritation there is more and more distance until the relationship falls apart.

> Reconciliation can be achieved if we follow biblical principles.

Relationships need not follow this pattern. Reconciliation can be achieved if we follow biblical principles. In Matthew 5:23-26 the Lord Jesus Christ provides us with the principles needed to repair relationships that we have damaged. When we have damaged a relationship with another person, we need to do what is necessary to achieve reconciliation. Two steps are necessary.

Admit Guilt

The first step to repairing a damaged relationship is to admit guilt and take responsibility for our actions. This is clear in verses 23 and 24:

> Therefore if you bring your gift to the altar, and there remember that your brother has something against you, leave your gift there before the altar, and go your way. First be reconciled to your brother, and then come and offer your gift.

When Convicted

Steps toward reconciliation should be taken immediately upon remembering that we have offended someone. If our conscience is operating rightly, it will accuse us when we are guilty (John 8:9;

Rom.2:15). As someone once said, "Your conscience may not keep you from doing wrong, but it keeps you from enjoying it." Some folks never seem to admit doing wrong. When confronted, they either claim they didn't mean to offend or they accuse the offended party of being overly sensitive.

Those who do not admit sin may do so for three reasons. Some have personality types that find it hard to admit a mistake. Others have a poor self-concept and compensate by never admitting a fault. Still others are motivated by pride and just will not humble themselves. Everyone needs to be able to admit guilt both to themselves and to others.

We must not excuse ourselves for the above reasons. The repeated refusal to acknowledge guilt will render our conscience insensitive. Once our conscience ceases to function correctly, we are in grave danger; our moral rudder is gone.

Before We Worship

It is not unusual to be confronted with our sin when we come to worship God. Jesus spoke of just such an occurrence in Matthew 5:23. At this point in time, the Old Testament Mosaic law was still operative. They worshipped God by offering animal sacrifices. Here, Jesus was anticipating offenders bringing a trespass offering to God while neglecting reconciliation on the human level. Therefore, He instructed them to dispense with their worship until they were reconciled with the one they had offended.

Reconciliation should precede worship.

How often we attempt to worship God while we are estranged from a fellow believer! What if Jesus Himself were to meet us at the front door of the church next Sunday? Would He invite us in to worship or send us away to be reconciled to a brother we had offended? Reconciliation should precede worship. Upon becoming aware of any offense committed against a brother, reconciliation should become our first priority.

To the Offended Party

We must confess our sins to the Lord, not as a means of maintaining salvation, but in order to please God and avoid His loving discipline. The word confess in 1 John 1:9 carries the basic idea of agreement. We have to agree with God's assessment of every thought, word, or action. If sin is against God and no other person, then confession to God is all that is needed. No one else needs to know.

It is often not enough, however, to confess our sins to God alone. James 5:16 says, "Confess your trespasses to one another …" Obviously this does not mean that every sin must be confessed publicly. But when a sin affects another human being, we must confess that sin to the one we have offended. This is what James indicates in this verse—in fact, a different form of the word *confess* appears in James 5:16 than does in 1 John 1:9. In James, the word that is used specifically refers to open or public confession before other people in addition to God.

Man has been excusing his sin since the very beginning. Adam tried to shift the blame to Eve, and Eve to the serpent (Gen. 3:12-13). We often use such excuses as "I'm under a lot of stress" and "I don't feel well." One major excuse in today's society is, "I was abused as a child." Excuses may point to real and even tragic circumstances in our past, but they never excuse us from what we choose to do in the present. Isaac, Joseph, and Daniel all turned out well, but each could have used his past as an excuse. Isaac could have forsaken God and blamed it on his father's trying to kill him. Joseph, sold by his brothers, might have turned bitter. Daniel, kidnapped at a tender age, could have denied his God with good excuse.

> **Man has been excusing his sin since the very beginning.**

Confession of sin does not come easy for fallen men, but it is essential to our spiritual health in general and our relationships in particular. As Proverbs 28:13 says, "He who covers his sins will not prosper, but whoever confesses and forsakes them will have mercy." Admitting our guilt is the first step to repairing any relationship we have damaged.

Make Amends

The second step to repairing a relationship is to make amends for our offense. Confession is necessary, but it is often not enough. If some material or physical damage has been done, an attempt to repair the damage (or at least the expense of it) should be made. The Mosaic law contained provisions for restitution, and this was what Jesus had in mind in Matthew 5:25-26.

> "Agree with your adversary quickly, while you are on the way with him, lest your adversary deliver you to the judge, the judge hand you over to the officer, and you be thrown into prison. Assuredly, I say to you, you will by no means get out of there till you have paid the last penny."

Willingly and Quickly

We must take the initiative to bring about reconciliation and do so as quickly as possible. Roman law allowed a plaintiff to forcibly bring the accused with him to court. Verse 25 says to agree with an adversary quickly, while "on the way." This means coming to an agreement before reaching the courtroom. We should settle any matter in which we are at fault out of court promptly paying whatever is owed. Settling a matter may only require a specific apology that acknowledges the pain we have caused. Offering a gift may also be a means of achieving an agreement. This is what Jacob did for Esau when he returned to the land (Gen. 32-33). Most wives would testify that flowers and chocolate go a long ways toward achieving reconciliation!

Sometimes, renewed commitments are what's needed, both expressed and demonstrated. John the Baptist asked those coming to him for baptism to bear fruits worthy of repentance (Luke 3:8). After Peter's denial of Jesus, the Lord told him to feed His sheep (John 21:17). Actual payment for damages or payment in excess of them may be what's required. The case of Zacchaeus, the chief tax collector who returned four-fold to those he had cheated, is a good example for us to follow, even though we are not subject to the specific Old Testament laws that he was (Luke 19:1-10).

Lest We Suffer the Consequences

We should make whatever amends are necessary in view of the possible consequences. In Jesus' day, offenders could end up in prison. There they would remain until they had paid all that was owed. This was not a pleasant proposition! Today, we need not fear imprisonment, but huge monetary awards may be ordered in civil cases. Without question, it is wise to avoid such a possibility.

Conclusion

When we have offended someone, repairing that relationship requires admitting guilt and making amends. Reconciliation certainly benefits the one we have offended, but it is also beneficial to us. We will be able to worship God with a clear conscience and avoid any costly consequences of our offense. And who can measure the value of a friendship salvaged? As Martha Mason put it, "The richest man in the world is not the one who still has the first dollar he ever earned—it's the man who still has his first friend."[4]

LESSON 1 EXAM

Use the answer sheet that has been provided to complete your exam.

1. **Interpersonal relationships are**
    A. more trouble than they are worth.
    B. vital for the wellbeing of every person.
    C. optional for those who want them.
    D. something that will draw you away from God.

2. **In which of the following passages did Jesus tell us how to reconcile difficult relationships?**
    A. 1 John 1:9   C. Luke 3:8
    B. Matthew 5:23-26   D. Mark 10:17-22

3. **The first step to repairing a damaged relationship is to**
    A. analyze the steps leading up to the separation.
    B. confront the person we have hurt with his guilt.
    C. wait for a while to see if things resolve themselves.
    D. admit guilt and take responsibility for our actions.

4. **Refusing to take responsibility for our offenses against others**
    A. desensitizes our conscience.
    B. helps us cope with our sinful nature.
    C. soothes our conscience.
    D. demonstrates good self-control.

5. **According to Jesus, at what point should we try to make things right with someone we've sinned against?**
    A. When they bring up the offense.
    B. When we are sure they actually were offended.
    C. When we can't keep quiet about it anymore.
    D. Immediately after we realize we've offended them.

6. **Why should we continually confess our sins to the Lord?**
    A. To maintain our salvation.
    B. To earn God's favor.
    C. To please God and avoid His loving discipline.
    D. To avoid eternal judgment.

7. **What does the word "confess" mean in 1 John 1:9?**
   A. Tell all the details to a church leader.
   B. Explain to God why you did what you did.
   C. Wallow in grief over what you did.
   D. Agree with God that what you did was sin.

8. **When is it enough to confess our sin to God and no one else?**
   A. When the offended person is no longer speaking to us.
   B. When the person offended lives far away.
   C. When our sin is against God alone.
   D. When it's a minor offense.

9. **We must try to bring about reconciliation**
   A. when the offended one comes to us.
   B. as quickly as possible.
   C. as soon as the problem becomes known to the church.
   D. when others pressure us to do so.

10. **The story of Zacchaeus in Luke 19 illustrates the biblical principle of making amends. Which of the following is a good example of that for us?**
    A. Offering a nonspecific apology to avoid bringing up the pain.
    B. Paying for damages, maybe even extra.
    C. Avoiding a renewed commitment.
    D. Promising anything to get the person to forgive you.

What Do You Say?

What have you learned about the relationship between forgiveness and physical health?

LESSON 2

When We Have Been Offended

America's number one health problem is not heart disease or cancer. In fact, it's not even physical in nature. According to Christian psychologists Frank Minrith and Paul Meier, *depression* is America's number one health problem. In their book *Happiness Is a Choice,* Minrith and Meier note the scope of the problem:

> A *majority* of Americans suffer from a serious, clinical depression at some time during their lives. At the present time, one American in twenty is medically diagnosed as suffering from depression. Of course, many more are depressed but never receive help. According to one estimate, about twenty million persons in America between the ages of eighteen and seventy-four are currently depressed.[5]

Minrith and Meier describe depression as anger turned inward (p. 99). They even go so far as to say that dealing with anger in the proper way can actually prevent clinical depression (p. 151). It is no wonder that Paul tells us not to let the sun go down on our wrath (Eph. 4:26). Obviously we can express anger in many sinful ways that should be avoided. However, when we repress anger rather than expressing it appropriately, it can lead to depression. It is just as sinful to hurt ourselves through depression as it is to hurt others through retaliation. There is an appropriate response to anger that lies between these two extremes.

Unfortunately, the fear of conflict hinders many from dealing directly with offenses. It needs to be understood that conflict is not bad. It may be unpleasant at times, especially to certain personality types, but it is not necessarily sinful. Dr. Terry Wise makes this point in the introduction to his book *Conflict Scenarios.*

Handled in the right manner, conflict can actually be positive and healthy. Yet because our behavior during conflict is often ungodly, we equate conflict with sin. But the truth of the matter is that disagreement is not sinful; how we act and react in a conflict situation can be. You like pepperoni pizza and I like sausage pizza—that is not sin. You like contemporary music while I prefer traditional sounds—that is not sin. But when I malign you for not agreeing with me, that is sin.[6]

As Dr. Wise indicates, conflict can be positive and healthy. It was conflict that led to the appointment of the first deacons (Acts 6). Without conflict, Barnabas could not have reclaimed John Mark (Acts 15:39). And Peter would have continued in his hypocrisy if Paul had not rebuked him (Gal. 2:11, 14).

Avoiding conflict is not the answer, because often conflict is the only way to solve a problem. We need to deal appropriately with our anger by dealing directly with those who offend us. In fact, when we have been offended, we are obligated to seek reconciliation with the offender. The teaching of the Lord Jesus in Matthew 18:15-17 provides us with the specifics. Notice that seeking reconciliation involves a three-step process.

Confront Privately

The first step in seeking reconciliation when we have been offended is to confront the offender privately. Notice verse 15:

> Moreover if your brother sins against you, go and tell him his fault between you and him alone. If he hears you, you have gained your brother.

Go to Them

Note that if a fellow believer sins against us, we are obligated to go to them. The verb *sins* means literally "to miss the mark" or "to be in error." If a brother commits a sin against us, we must go to him. Any offense should be handled this way. The command to go is in the present tense, and it is in the imperative mode. In other words, we have an ever present obligation to go to an offender. We are commanded to go, at all times, whenever we are offended.

Show Them Their Sin

The purpose of going to them is obviously to confront the offender with his or her sin. The matter in question should be dealt with privately, "between you and him alone." If the offender responds by admitting his sin and asking for forgiveness (if he hears), then we gain a brother. What Christ says in the gospel of Luke gives us the same advice. He says to rebuke the offender and to forgive him, if he repents (Luke 17:3). Unfortunately, we often react in a number of ways that contrast with biblical confrontation. As already mentioned, we can remain silent and repress our anger, opening the door to depression. This type of reaction to offense is often accompanied by avoiding the offender. As a result of isolation, we lose the benefit of our relationship with the offender.

Another reaction involves openly expressing one's anger and refusing to forgive the offender. When we hold such a grudge and refuse to forgive, we rob ourselves of God's parental forgiveness (Matt. 6:14-15). Finally, we may resort to sarcasm, become overly critical, or engage in character assassination. Strife and factions may develop as others take sides in the matter. We certainly need to avoid these human reactions and respond properly to offenses.

> **When we refuse to forgive, we rob ourselves of God's parental forgiveness.**

There are many good reasons for biblical confrontation. First, the offending party may be unaware of his offense. In such cases, confrontation is necessary to produce an awareness of the offense and bring about an appropriate apology. Second, a misunderstanding may have occurred. We may have been offended at what we *thought* was said, when in fact we misunderstood the other person's words. Confrontation allows for misunderstandings to be cleared up.

A third reason for confrontation is that a face-to-face airing of grievances diffuses tension. Confrontation that has reconciliation as its goal is a conciliatory act. Fourth, confrontation forces both parties to articulate their grievances. When we hold a grudge, we usually perceive the offense to be greater than it really was but when we are forced to articulate a specific grievance, the reverse can occur. Positive confrontation can make mountains into molehills. Finally, confrontation dramatically increases the chances of reconciliation. Without it, how could we expect to resolve interpersonal conflicts?

When we confront others, we should always be gentle. Galatians 6:1 tells us that we should restore those overtaken in any trespass while exhibiting a spirit of gentleness. It is good to be inquisitive rather than accusing toward a brother. It is better to ask what another person meant by a certain comment than to accuse them of malicious intent. In this way one can address another person's sin in a gentle manner.

Work to Achieve Reconciliation

Reconciliation is always the goal of private confrontation. The Lord Jesus says of the offender, "If he hears you, you have gained your brother." The desired response of the one who truly hears us is repentance and reconciliation. However, we may encounter a negative response. The offender may deny any wrongdoing, become defensive, offer an excuse, or shift the blame to someone else. Invariably, anger and accusation accompany negative responses.

Reconciliation is always the goal of private confrontation.

Perhaps as a smoke screen, the offender who is confronted makes the act of confrontation itself out to be an offense. This is an all too common occurrence. I once confronted a widow who had all but ceased to attend worship services. She had previously been very faithful in her attendance, but had often been absent since beginning to date a man in our community. After lovingly expressing my concern about her misplaced priorities, she promptly left the church and told everyone that I had offended her. In fact, she told everyone that I had hurt her more than anyone had ever hurt her. Such responses require that we take a second step in seeking reconciliation.

Confront with Witnesses

The second step in seeking reconciliation is to confront an offender in the presence of witnesses. Notice verse 16:

> "But if he will not hear, take with you one or two more, that 'by the mouth of two or three witnesses every word may be established.'"

Enlist Help

Although these other parties are called "witnesses," we should not assume that they serve only to confirm the offender's sin so that church discipline can be effectively administered. Their function is to help bring about reconciliation. It is the offended party's responsibility to select witnesses and to try again to achieve reconciliation.

The Benefit of Witnesses

Witnesses are beneficial for several reasons. They can bring additional pressure on the offender to repent, by their words or merely by their presence. They can also act as arbitrators when the need for restitution is agreed upon, but its extent is in dispute. Finally, if reconciliation is not achieved, they will be able to confirm the offended parties' efforts at reconciliation. This will become necessary when the third step is taken. Those who are reluctant to get involved in personal disputes should consider Matthew 5:9: "Blessed are the peacemakers, for they shall be called sons of God."

Confront Publicly

The third step in seeking reconciliation is to confront offenders publicly. Note verse 17:

> "And if he refuses to hear them, tell it to the church. But if he refuses even to hear the church, let him be to you like a heathen and a tax collector."

Go Before the Church

Telling the church means bringing the matter before the assembly for a decision. As believers we are commanded not to take another believer to a secular court. Paul warned the Corinthian church about this very thing in 1 Corinthians 6:1, "Dare any of you, having a matter against another, go to law before the unrighteous, and not before the saints?" Instead, we are to bring the matter before the church body.

Allow Time for Repentance

Telling the church is not an act of expulsion at this point. Unfortunately, it is often viewed as such. A meeting is called, the congregation informed, and before the meeting is adjourned, a vote is taken to exclude the offender. But Jesus says, "Tell it to the church" followed by, "But if he refuses even to hear the church ..." An offender's refusal to hear even the church implies that he is given the opportunity to repent. As Marshall Shelly says in his book *Well Intentioned Dragons,* "Telling the church is not punishment, it is enlisting the help of the whole body in reconciliation."[7] The church as a whole brings added pressure on the offender to repent. Time is required for this process to work.

Suspend the Relationship

Only after the offender refuses to hear the church should discipline be exercised. The unrepentant offender is to be considered "like a heathen and a tax collector." In other words, he is to be treated as if he were an unbeliever. A "tax collector" was a Jew, who had become an outcast due to his profession—collecting taxes for the Romans. Tax collectors typically collected an excess of what was owed and pocketed the difference.

> **These steps outlined by Jesus are not optional.**

When church discipline is finally exercised, it is incumbent on all within the body to cease their association with the offender. He becomes an outcast, but for good reason. Compare the words of the apostle Paul to the Thessalonians, "And if anyone does not obey our word in this epistle, note that person and do not keep company with him, that he may be ashamed" (2 Thess. 3:14). Notice that the severed relationships have a positive purpose and are not simply a means of punishing the offender. There is still the possibility of repentance resulting from the shame of isolation.

Conclusion

Jesus taught that we need to confront offenders and seek reconciliation. Furthermore, these steps outlined by Jesus are not optional. Throughout this passage, Jesus used imperative verbs. We are commanded to confront offenders privately, take witnesses, and finally tell the church. These steps must be followed if there is to be any hope of reconciliation.

LESSON 2 EXAM

Use the answer sheet that has been provided to complete your exam.

1. **"When we repress anger rather than expressing it appropriately, it can lead to**
   A. spreading gossip."
   B. depression."
   C. pride."
   D. low self-esteem."

2. **Conflict**
   A. can be positive and healthy.
   B. is always sinful.
   C. always creates ill-will.
   D. always results in anger.

3. **When we have been offended we must**
   A. seek reconciliation with the offender.
   B. ostracize the offender.
   C. maintain our anger against the offender.
   D. tell everyone of the offense.

4. **What does the word *sin* mean?**
   A. To do something horrible or violent.
   B. To miss the mark or to be in error.
   C. To do something that only hurts someone else, not myself.
   D. To be completely taken over by Satan.

5. **Which of the following is a good reason for private, biblical confrontation?**
   A. We can vent anger without upsetting anyone else besides the offender.
   B. We can temporarily repress our anger.
   C. It's a way of making mountains out of molehills.
   D. Articulating our grievances can clear up misunderstandings.

6. **Which of the following is a good example of confronting an offender with gentleness?**
   A. Accusing the offender clearly and forcefully.
   B. Speaking with a soft voice.
   C. Asking an offender what he meant by a comment.
   D. Asking why the person did what he did.

7. **What outcome should we look for when we confront those who have sinned against us?**
   A. Proof that we were right and they were wrong.
   B. An immediate loving feeling toward them.
   C. Deep emotion so we know they are sincere.
   D. Repentance and reconciliation.

8. **If the offender doesn't respond to private confrontation, what is one benefit of taking witnesses the next time you meet with him or her?**
   A. You'll have more people "on your side."
   B. The offender will feel intimidated.
   C. The witnesses won't leave until they get a confession.
   D. The witnesses can verify that you tried to restore the relationship.

9. **Telling the church allows for**
   A. an opportunity to punish the offender.
   B. others to help in attaining reconciliation.
   C. a judicial decision to expel him from the church.
   D. everyone to know his attitude.

10. **Our last resort is to sever ties with a person who refuses to admit his wrong. What is the goal of this isolation?**
    A. To punish wrongdoing.
    B. To ultimately bring about repentance.
    C. To prove who's right and who's wrong.
    D. To avoid relationships with sinful people.

What Do You Say?

Have you ever been offended by a fellow Christian? Did you follow these steps to reconciliation? What was the result?

_____

_____

_____

_____

LESSON 3

When Offenders Repent

Karen Linamen wrote about her refusal to forgive her husband in an issue of *Today's Christian Woman.* What she shares about carrying a grudge she calls first-hand experience!

> A grudge usually has a legitimate beginning. Someone we trust—an acquaintance, friend, or family member—does something that causes us pain, and we feel hurt. Too often, we conclude: If I have a right to feel hurt, then I must have the right to feel hurt for a very, very, very long time. The trouble is, feeling hurt for a very, very, very long time doesn't damage the person who hurt us as much as it damages you and me. Grudges deplete our energy, isolate us from others, and keep old wounds from healing. They increase tension and stress in our life. They compromise our joy, disrupt our sleep, and harden our heart, if not arteries.[8]

Besides the emotional toll extracted by an unforgiving spirit, there are other consequences. Scientific studies of those who refuse to forgive being done at the University of Tennessee by Drs. Warren Jones and Kathleen Lawler have identified two interesting results. One is physical in nature. Lawler says, "Those who had been unable to forgive friends or partners reported more health problems." In this study, they have actually measured during interviews an increase in blood pressure of those who were carrying a grudge.

The second result they report is increased loneliness. "There's something about forgiveness that helps us maintain satisfying reciprocal adult relationships," says Lawler.[9] Is your circle of friends shrinking year by year? Are you lonely? Are you experiencing increased stress, tension and poor health? If so, it may be that you are unwilling to forgive. If such serious consequences result from an unwillingness to forgive, it's no wonder God tells us in His Word to forgive every offender that repents!

Forgiving offenders who acknowledge their sin is not an option. Jesus' teaching in Matthew 18:21-35 makes it clear that we must forgive everyone that seeks forgiveness.

Every Time They Repent

We must forgive everyone that repents *every time* they acknowledge their sin and request forgiveness. Consider the words of Jesus in verses 21 and 22:

> Then Peter came to Him and said, "Lord, how often shall my brother sin against me, and I forgive him? Up to seven times?" Jesus said to him, "I do not say to you, up to seven times, but up to seventy times seven."

Without Setting Limits

Peter was being generous when he posed his question. Jewish rabbis limited the duty to forgive to only three times. After forgiving someone three times, doing so a fourth time was not required. Peter stretched the figure to seven in his question, but Jesus wasn't impressed. Instead, he told Peter to forgive seventy times seven. It is unclear in the original whether seventy plus seven is meant or seventy times seven. Be it seventy-seven or 490, the meaning is the same. Our willingness to forgive should not be limited.

The offender's acknowledgement of sin and his request for forgiveness is, of course, assumed. Notice Luke 17:3 in this regard: "Take heed to yourselves. If your brother sins against you, rebuke him; and if he repents, forgive him." The word *repent* means "to have a change of mind." In this case it indicates a change of mind about a "sin." An offender who once refused to confess a sin is said to "repent" when he decides to admit his sin and seek forgiveness.

Those who refuse to forgive may offer one or more excuses. They may claim that an offender has hurt them too many times. It is clear from these verses that such an excuse is not legitimate. They may claim that the offense was too great to forgive. This too involves an arbitrary limit set by the offended party and is without precedent in the Scriptures.

Some may argue that to forgive an offender would be equivalent to

WHEN OFFENDERS REPENT **25**

condoning his sin. This, too, is absurd, since forgiveness is conditioned on repentance, and repentance involves an acknowledgment of one's sin. Finally, some fear that forgiveness somehow gives an offender permission to hurt them again. This is not the case. Again, the requirement of repentance provides the necessary assurance.

> **Forgiving someone requires a decision to never again make an issue of the offense.**

Excuses aside, forgiveness may be legitimately withheld until repentance is proven to be genuine. John the Baptist required such proof when he warned the multitudes that came to him to "bear fruits worthy of repentance."

Marie Williams provides us with a practical illustration of how repentance may be confirmed.[10] In her firsthand account she tells of separating from her husband after years of drug abuse and repeated episodes of violence. Several months after their separation, her husband showed up at church, rededicated his life to Christ, and asked to be baptized. Faced with his apparent repentance she would have to forgive him, but was he sincere? She still feared for her daughter's safety and wellbeing. After much prayer, she decided to wait and see while remaining separated for three months. She determined to accept his transformation if he was still attending church after the three months and bearing fruits worthy of repentance. Within three weeks he returned to his old lifestyle. We must always be willing to forgive without setting limits, but proof of repentance is sometimes necessary.

Not Making Past Offenses an Issue

Forgiving someone requires a decision to never again make an issue of his or her offense. The word *forgive* means "to dismiss or send away." An appropriate mental picture would be releasing a helium-filled balloon. The one who possesses the balloon chooses to release it and it floats up and away, out of sight, gone forever. Forgiveness is the choice to dismiss an offense. It is a decision. It involves a person's will, but not necessarily their emotions.

The choice to forgive does not require the re-establishment of the same emotional closeness as existed before the offense. In time, an offender may regain the trust of the offended party along with the same measure of emotional closeness that existed before the offense, but forgiveness should precede—not follow—this process. It involves a commitment to never bring up a past offense or let it ever again become an issue in the relationship.

Clara Barton, the famous American Civil War nurse, reportedly never held a grudge against anyone. One time, a friend reminded her of a cruel thing that had been done to her years before, but Clara seemed not to remember the incident. "Don't you remember the wrong that was done you?" her friend asked. To which Clara replied, "No, I distinctly remember forgetting that."[11] Forgiveness, indeed, is a matter of choice.

In Order to Be Forgiven

We must forgive everyone that repents every time they acknowledge their sin, and we must do so in order to receive forgiveness ourselves. To make this additional point, Jesus related a parable.

Positional Forgiveness

The born-again believer already possesses judicial forgiveness (Rom. 8:1). In regard to his eternal destiny, his sins have been forever forgiven. God will never bring them up again (Heb. 10:17). The penalty for sin was extracted at the cross of Christ (2 Cor. 5:21). The only condition to eternal forgiveness is faith in Christ (Rom. 3:21-26), at which point the believer is granted eternal life (John 3:16). This is what is represented by the forgiveness granted to the servant in the first part of the parable in Matthew 18:23-27:

> Therefore the kingdom of heaven is like a certain king who wanted to settle accounts with his servants. And when he had begun to settle accounts, one was brought to him who owed him ten thousand talents. But as he was not able to pay, his master commanded that he be sold, with his wife and children and all that he had, and that payment be made. The servant therefore fell down before him, saying, "Master, have patience with me, and I will pay you all." Then the master of that servant was moved with compassion, released him, and forgave him the debt.

The servant in question owed his lord ten thousand talents. He was evidently an overseer for an ancient ruler. When it came time to settle up with his master, he owed the king a huge sum that he had collected but evidently squandered. The amount was so large that he could not possibly repay it. A *talent* was equal to six thousand denari. A denarius was a Roman coin that was worth a day's wage for the common laborer. The ten thousand talents, what the servant owed, would have been equal to six thousand denari times ten thousand, or sixty million denari! Sixty million denari divided by 365 days would equal a common laborer's wage for 164,384 years. Even assuming a long life span of eighty years, this amount would represent all a man could earn in 2,055 lifetimes! Repayment of such a sum was impossible, but this man's master had compassion on him and forgave the enormous debt. This is akin to what God does for every lost sinner who repents. He forgives a debt of sin that cannot be paid by the sinner. God Himself in the person of Christ made the payment and absorbed the loss on the cross of Calvary (2 Cor. 5:19). Every sinner who repents receives judicial forgiveness full and free.

Relational Forgiveness

Although positionally forgiven, believers need forgiveness from God on a day-to-day basis in order to maintain a favorable "family" relationship with Him (1 John 1:9). Otherwise, God, as their heavenly Father, will be displeased with their behavior and chasten them (Heb. 12:6). His chastening is always for the purpose of correction—never punishment. The result of this kind of forgiveness is the avoidance of God's correction. There are two conditions for such forgiveness: we need to confess sin (1 John 1:9) and we need to forgive those who have offended us (Matt. 6:14-15). The latter condition is the point of verses 28 to 35 of Matthew 18:

> "But that servant went out and found one of his fellow servants who owed him a hundred denari; and he laid hands on him and took him by the throat, saying, 'Pay me what you owe!' So his fellow servant fell down at his feet and begged him, saying, 'Have patience with me, and I will pay you all.' And he would not, but went and threw him into prison till he should pay the debt. So when his fellow servants saw what had been done, they were very grieved, and came and told their master all that had been done. Then his master, after he had called him, said to him, 'You wicked servant! I forgave you all that debt because you begged me. Should you not also have had compassion on your fellow servant, just as I had pity on you?' And his master was angry, and delivered him to the torturers until he should pay all that was due to him. So My heavenly Father also will do to you if each of you, from his heart, does not forgive his brother his trespasses."

The same servant who was forgiven a huge debt that he could never repay refused to forgive a fellow servant a comparatively small sum. The amount was one hundred denari, or the wages that could be earned in one hundred days. Although this was not an insignificant sum, it was certainly a manageable debt and a trivial one in comparison to his astronomical debt that was cancelled.

However, he did not extend the same compassion to his fellow servant. As Roman law allowed, he took the debtor by the throat and demanded payment. When this was reported to the unforgiving servant's lord, he was angry and rescinded his earlier decision to forgive the servant's debt. Jesus interpreted the meaning of the parable plainly in verse 35. Our heavenly Father will not forgive those who refuse to forgive.

> **Our heavenly Father will not forgive those who refuse to forgive.**

Conclusion

Indeed, we must forgive everyone who sincerely seeks our forgiveness. It is often difficult, but always a matter of obedience and always beneficial.

> Years after her concentration camp experiences in Nazi Germany, Corrie ten Boon met face-to-face one of the most cruel and heartless German guards that she had ever contacted. He had humiliated and degraded her and her sister. He had jeered and visually raped them as they stood in the delousing shower. Now he stood before her with hand outstretched and said, "Will you forgive me?" She writes: "I stood there with coldness clutching at my heart, but I know that the will can function regardless of the temperature of the heart. I prayed, Jesus help me! Woodenly, mechanically I thrust my hand into the one stretched out to me and I experienced an incredible thing. The current started in my shoulder, raced down my arms and sprang into our clutched hands. Then this warm reconciliation seemed to flood my whole being, bringing tears to my eyes. 'I forgive you, brother,' I cried with my whole heart. For a long moment we grasped each other's hands, the former guard, the former prisoner. I have never known the love of God so intensely as I did that moment!"[12]

May we also experience such intense love.

LESSON 3 EXAM

Use the answer sheet that has been provided to complete your exam.

1. **Holding a grudge**
   A. greatly damages the one who caused the hurt.
   B. is the best way to encourage repentance.
   C. damages the one holding the grudge more than the one who hurt him.
   D. decreases the likelihood of further hurt.

2. **Which of the following was Jesus' main point in saying we need to forgive "seventy times seven"?**
   A. It's important to "keep score."
   B. When someone has offended us 491 times, we don't have to forgive anymore.
   C. Our willingness to forgive should not be limited.
   D. A person can only take so much!

3. **Luke 17:3 says, "If your brother sins against you, rebuke him: and if he repents, forgive him." What is repentance?**
   A. Explaining to God why you did what you did.
   B. Making a 180-degree turn from making excuses for sin, to admitting our sin and seeking forgiveness.
   C. Making a tearful confession.
   D. Repeatedly asking God for forgiveness.

4. **Forgiving someone requires**
   A. being able to totally forget about it.
   B. a special giftedness.
   C. a loving feeling toward the offender.
   D. a decision to never make an issue of the offense again.

5. **According to Romans 3:21-26, the only condition for our eternal forgiveness is**
   A. living a life free from sin.
   B. doing more good deeds than bad deeds in our lifetime.
   C. faith in Christ.
   D. keeping the Ten Commandments.

6. **Judicial forgiveness means that if we place our faith in Christ,**
   A. God has forgiven us because Christ paid the penalty for our sins on the cross.
   B. God will never bring up our sins again.
   C. Our "position" before Him is secure: we are eternally forgiven.
   D. All of the above.

7. **What is the term for the forgiveness we receive when we confess our sins daily in order to maintain a close relationship with God?**
   A. Relational forgiveness
   B. Positional forgiveness
   C. Judicial forgiveness
   D. Conditional forgiveness

8. **God's chastening is always for the purpose of**
   A. punishment.
   B. humiliation.
   C. rebuking.
   D. correction.

9. **According to 1 John 1:9 and Matthew 6:14-15, what are the two conditions for receiving God's day-to-day forgiveness?**
   A. Expressing our sorrow and paying some sort of penance.
   B. Confessing our sin to God and forgiving those who have offended us.
   C. Asking for forgiveness from God and from the whole church.
   D. Admitting our sins before the church and trying to forgive the person who hurt us.

10. **Forgiving everyone who sincerely seeks our forgiveness is**
    A. easy.
    B. impossible.
    C. optional.
    D. a matter of obedience to Christ.

What Do You Say?

How can you apply the story about Clara Barton to some situation in your life?

LESSON 4

When Offenders Do Not Repent

Everett Worthington Jr. is described as a psychologist, marriage counselor, and recognized authority on the subject of forgiveness in an article published in 1999 by the *Knoxville News-Sentinel*.[13] Worthington is a member of the faculty at Virginia Commonwealth University, and he has spent many years overseeing graduate students' research on the topic of forgiveness. He has also authored or co-authored over a dozen books on the topic and presently heads the Campaign for Forgiveness Research, a nonprofit organization that funds scientific research on forgiveness. The article describes a personal crisis in Worthington's life that challenged what he knew and believed about forgiveness:

> When his telephone rang on New Year's Day 1996, his personal understanding of forgiveness was shaken to its roots. His brother, Mike Worthington, who still lives in Knoxville, was calling with shattering news. Mike had found their widowed mother, Frances Worthington, beaten to death that morning, a victim of one or more attackers who had broken into her home on Price Avenue in South Knoxville.[14]

Later, upon hearing the brutal details of his mother's death, the same article records his own description of his reaction:

> I saw my nephew's baseball bat propped up in the corner of my brother's house, and I remember saying, "I wish I had whoever did this here right now. I would take that baseball bat and beat them to death." I was furious. It was a difficult situation.[15]

Worthington's reaction was a natural human response. In some degree, we have all experienced a similar desire for vengeance of one kind or another. However, we are not free to act on such desires. We have scriptural examples to the contrary. Jesus, when He was being crucified, prayed, "Father, forgive them, for they do not know what they do" (Luke 23:34). As Stephen was being stoned he cried, "Lord, do not charge them with this sin" (Acts 7:60). In neither case was there any repentance at that time on the part of those forgiven. Yet in Luke 17:3, Jesus said, "If your brother sins against you, rebuke him; and if he repents, forgive him." According to this verse, forgiveness requires repentance. How can we reconcile Luke 17:3 with the previous examples?

Obviously, two different situations are in view. We are obligated to forgive those who repent. And it follows that this requires a complete restoration of the relationship. But what of those who do not repent, such as those who crucified Jesus or stoned Stephen? We cannot forgive them in the same way, but we do have certain obligations.

In a limited sense, we are obligated to forgive everyone who offends us but who does not acknowledge doing so. Romans 12:17-21 identifies our responsibility in such a case. We have two specific obligations.

Do Them No Harm

Our first obligation toward an unrepentant offender involves not trying to get even. Consider Paul's words in verses 17 through 19:

> Repay no one evil for evil. Have regard for good things in the sight of all men. If it is possible, as much as depends on you, live peaceably with all men. Beloved, do not avenge yourselves, but, rather give place to wrath; for it is written, "Vengeance is Mine, I will repay," says the Lord.

Don't Repay Evil for Evil

We are not to return evil for evil as if we were repaying a debt. The word *repay* means to "fulfill an obligation or repay a debt" and is often used to refer to human or divine retribution. The admonition, "Have regard for good things in the sight of all men," is not a change of subject, but refers to our public testimony when we refrain from getting even. The word translated "good" means to be outwardly free of defect, to be noble or praiseworthy. The NIV translates this verse, "Be careful to do what is right in the eyes of everybody." The meaning is clear. We should maintain a good testimony by refusing to repay evil for evil.

Thus far, Paul has emphasized our obligation in two ways. Now he adds a third admonition. He says that we should endeavor to "live peaceably with all men." Each of these admonitions contains present-tense imperative verbs.

God commands us not to return evil for evil at any time. Jesus Himself said in Matthew 5:38-39,

> "You have heard that it was said, 'An eye for an eye and a tooth for a tooth.' But I tell you not to resist an evil person. But whoever slaps you on your right cheek, turn the other to him also."

Leave Vengeance to God

When we choose not to get even, we are not dispensing with justice; we are simply leaving its execution to God. We are not to avenge ourselves. Instead, we are to allow God the opportunity. This is what Paul means when he tells us to "give place to wrath." We are to allow God the time and space to dispense His wrath. In support of his command, Paul draws upon Deuteronomy 32:35. Vengeance belongs to the Lord. The desire for revenge comes naturally. It is instinctive. It does not require a decision-making process. But leaving vengeance with God requires a conscious choice of the will.

In a limited sense, this is a decision to forgive an offender. However, forgiveness in this sense is not restorative. Restoration would require repentance. It is, rather, a unilateral choice by the offended party not to respond in kind to the evil that was done.

Everett Worthinton's story again illustrates the point. After his initial desire for revenge by beating his mother's killer to death, Worthington came to a decision to forgive. Later that night, unable to sleep, Worthington reflected on his mother's death

> **Leaving vengeance with God requires a conscious choice of the will.**

and the irony of being a researcher and counselor who had dealt with forgiveness for years.

> "Knowing that we had a method that hundreds of people had been able to use, I began to wonder, who did I write this book for? Was it for couples and other people who needed help? Or did I write this book for me? I think that night I was able to empathize and eventually come

to forgiveness. I know as a Christian if I confess my sin, I will be forgiven of it. And I know the relief that comes as a result. If I can feel this way by being forgiven, who am I to withhold such forgiveness from a person who harmed my Mom? At that point, I was able to release him. I haven't been burdened by that unforgiveness since then."[16]

In making a decision to forgive, Worthington advises making one's commitment to forgive tangible. If you make your forgiveness tangible, you are less likely to doubt it later. Tell a friend, partner, or counselor that you have forgiven the person who hurt you. Consider writing a "certificate of forgiveness," stating that you have, as of today, forgiven.

Be Kind to Them

Our second obligation to the unrepentant offender is kindness. We are to repay evil with kind deeds. Paul, calling to mind Proverbs 25:21-22, makes this clear:

> Therefore, "If your enemy is hungry, feed him; If he is thirsty, give him a drink; For in so doing you will heap coals of fire on his head." Do not be overcome by evil, but overcome evil with good.
>
> –Romans 12:20-21

Meet Their Needs

It is not enough to renounce getting even; we are obligated to repay evil with kindness. Paul puts it in very practical terms. We should meet their needs, whatever needs they have. If an enemy is hungry we should feed him. If an enemy is thirsty we should give him a drink. Any offender who has not repented has placed himself in an adversarial position. In a very real sense, he is an enemy and we owe him kindness. Both verbs ("feed" and "give drink") are imperatives, meaning that they are commands of God. Both are also present-tense verbs, meaning that we are continually under these obligations.

A Christian should be known for his benevolence toward those who mistreat him. Of English clergyman Thomas Cranmer it was said: "If you want to get a favor from him, do him a wrong." We should so live so that the same could be said of us.

To Produce Shame

The purpose of meeting our enemy's needs is stated in the latter part of verse 20. It is that, in so doing, we will "heap coals of fire on his head." At first thought, this sounds like vengeance of some sort. In reality, it is an appropriate way of producing guilt and shame over his previous mistreatment of an obviously kindhearted individual. John MacArthur explains that heaping coals of fire on someone's head refers to an Egyptian custom of demonstrating public contrition. He says that they would carry a pan of burning coals on their head to represent their burning pain of shame and guilt.[17] It is the believer's kindness that leads to this end.

In August of 1998, researcher Tamara Ferguson of Utah State University presented to the American Psychological Association the results of a study in which she asked 384 college students to recall instances when somebody made them feel guilty. An AP story by Malcolm Ritter provides us with the details.[18] She checked on three categories of technique. One involved direct assertions, saying, "That's not fair!" or, "Do you know what you've done?" A second included indirect ploys—giving hints through tone of voice. The third introduced the topic with apparent kindness: "It's all right, I forgive you"; or "It's not your fault"; or, "You don't need to make it up to me." When the students reported an incident that produced lingering guilt, the guilt trip was usually delivered through the kindness category. It is not repayment in kind that produces guilt, but rather kindness that is not deserved.

> It is not repayment in kind that produces guilt, but rather kindness that is not deserved.

Conclusion

Fulfilling these obligations is difficult because they run counter to our nature. But it is the only way we can effectively deal with an unrepentant offender. Let us therefore set aside all desires for vengeance and be kind to those who offend us.

LESSON 4 EXAM

Use the answer sheet that has been provided to complete your exam.

1. **When we experience a desire for vengeance,**
    A. we are free to act on it.
    B. we are not free to act on it.
    C. we must act on it immediately.
    D. we must wait for the best opportunity.

2. **Acts 7:60 tells us that _____ forgave his adversaries when he was being stoned.**
    A. Peter   C. James
    B. John   D. Stephen

3. **When someone repents of a sin against us**
    A. we have a choice whether or not to forgive him.
    B. we are obligated to forgive him.
    C. we probably should forgive him.
    D. we must take appropriate measures to punish him.

4. **Romans 12:17 tells us we should maintain a good testimony by**
    A. standing up for our rights.
    B. withdrawing from an evil environment.
    C. refusing to repay evil for evil.
    D. avoiding evil people.

5. **What does Paul say followers of Christ should do, as much as possible, in situations of conflict?**
    A. Avoid rocking the boat.
    B. Try to live peaceably with all the people around us.
    C. Use the conflict to set the record straight once and for all.
    D. Avoid the person altogether.

6. **When we choose not to get even we are**
    A. dispensing with justice.
    B. showing that we are weak.
    C. leaving vengeance to God.
    D. starting a new conflict.

7. **When making a decision to forgive, it is a good idea to**
    A. not tell anyone about it.
    B. inform the one who hurt you.
    C. to look closely into the offenders motives.
    D. tell someone that you have forgiven.

8. **How should we respond to someone who has hurt us and won't repent?**
    A. Show kindness by meeting their needs.
    B. Make them feel guilty about how much they've hurt us.
    C. Withhold kindness until they repent.
    D. Warn everyone about this person's tendency to hurt people.

9. **What should Christians be known for?**
    A. Their righteous indignation.
    B. Making everyone conform to biblical standards.
    C. Their kindness toward those who mistreat them.
    D. Their inability to feel anger when mistreated.

10. **What does Paul mean when he says being kind to the unrepentant offender is like heaping coals of fire on someone's head?**
    A. It's a picture of bringing shame that can eventually lead to repentance.
    B. It's a contradiction because burning coals would hurt the person.
    C. It's a symbol of being passionate in our denouncement of the person.
    D. It's a good way to literally make them sweat.

What Do You Say?

What are some practical ways you could show kindness to someone who has sinned against you but won't acknowledge that he's wrong?

_____

_____

_____

_____

Bibliography

[1] Paul Faulkner, *Making Things Right When Things Go Wrong* (West Monroe, LA: Howard Publishing, 1996), 155.

[2] *The USA Today*, June 14, 1999.

[3] John C. Maxwell, *Be a People Person* (Wheaton: Victor Books, 1989), 118-119.

[4] www.peerministry.org.

[5] Frank B. Minrith and Paul D. Meier, *Happiness Is a Choice* (Grand Rapids: Baker Book House, 1978), 22.

[6] Terry S. Wise, *Conflict Scenarios* (Needham Heights, MA: Simon & Schuster Custom Publishing, 1997), 15.

[7] Marshall Shelley, *Well-Intentioned Dragons* (Carol Stream, IL: Word Books, 1985), 131.

[8] Today's Christian Woman, July/Aug. 1999, 61.

[9] The Knoxville News-Sentinel, Aug. 24, 1999.

[10] Moody Monthly, July/Aug. 1999, 14.

[11] Paul Lee Tan, *Encyclopedia of 15,000 Illustrations* (Dallas: Bible Communications, 1998), 901.

[12] James S. Hewett, *Illustrations Unlimited* (Wheaton: Tyndale House Publishers, 1988), 218.

[13] The Knoxville News-Sentinel, July 24, 1999.

[14] Ibid.

[15] Ibid.

[16] Ibid.

[17] John MacArthur, *Romans 9-16* (Chicago: Moody Press, 1994), 203.

[18] The Charlotte Observer, Aug. 1998.